Pictographs

Chetro Ketl excavation

And don't forget fire. Fire has guided us since we first walked the earth. Signal fires from high points on the land could have been seen over vast distances. They could have helped direct people to Chaco. Roads later appeared. At Chaco, archeologists have located hundreds of miles of roads.

Did you know?

Chetro Ketl stands about 12 feet above the surrounding valley. Builders had to bring in tons of dirt and rock to elevate it to this height. Engineering was a hallmark of Chaco Culture.

Chaco Canyon is different.

If you have seen Mesa Verde, Aztec Ruins, or Canyon de Chelly you know that the ancestors stopped at these places during their migrations. They built homes and planted seeds. At Chaco Canyon, people did the same. They grew food, watered crops, and traded. But they also left behind buildings far different than any others before or since.

A.D. 400–500

Climate changes brought increased rain, making Chaco a popular place to grow corn, beans, and squash. People dug shallow pits in the earth, which they roofed with wood and plastered with mud so they could live close to their farmland. Homes at Chaco looked like other southwestern homes at the time.

Chacoan ladles

Casa Chiquita

Prehistoric steps

A.D. 700

The Chacoans began to build homes above ground, much like everyone else who lived around them.

A.D. 850-1150

Something happened at Chaco Canyon, something **REALLY DIFFERENT.** Who thought it up and why? People at Mesa Verde built homes high in the cliffs. At Casa Grande, people constructed buildings for elite community members. But nothing anywhere was like the grand architecture of Chaco Canyon. Here buildings are **BIG**.

Chacoan jars

Chaco had EVERYTHING

It had villages near a massive building now called a great house. It had villages that spread out across the land. Some villages surrounded a great kiva, a ceremonial building, while others had no great kiva. And Chaco had roads that seemed to lead everywhere. Chaco had something for everyone, much like our big cities today.

WHAT IF YOU HAD LIVED AT CHACO?

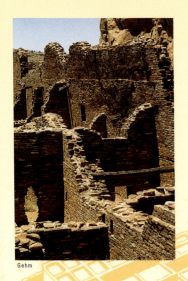

ENGINEER

You had a lot of responsibility. You designed buildings that stood **four** and sometimes **five stories high.** They contained hundreds of rooms. Engineers needed a lot of wood for roofing in a region with few trees. They also needed a massive number of hand-cut stones for the walls. Over time engineers created a consistent plan for the whole canyon.

CONSTRUCTION WORKER

You were not the first member of your family to work on a building. When you were a child, others laid the first stones. To finish Chetro Ketl, you and others like you quarried, cut, and placed approximately **50 million stones.** You used **5,000 trees** to roof it.

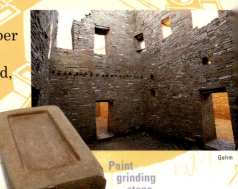

Paint grinding stone

Gehm (both)

Public Official

Buildings show what people think about themselves. They show the way they want others to see them. **As a public official, you worked with engineers** to make sure Chacoan buildings fit your view of the world. If the buildings were **BIG** they could shelter many travelers. And if they could shelter many travelers, people might come to Chaco from far away.

SUNWATCHERS

At Chaco, sunwatchers helped officials plan important ceremonies and the planting of crops. They watched where the sun appeared on the horizon throughout the year, especially at **solstice** or **equinox.** Certain windows, doors, and petroglyphs appear to have been used as time markers.

Fajada Butte time markers

Summer Solstice

Autumnal Equinox

Winter Solstice

Spring Equinox

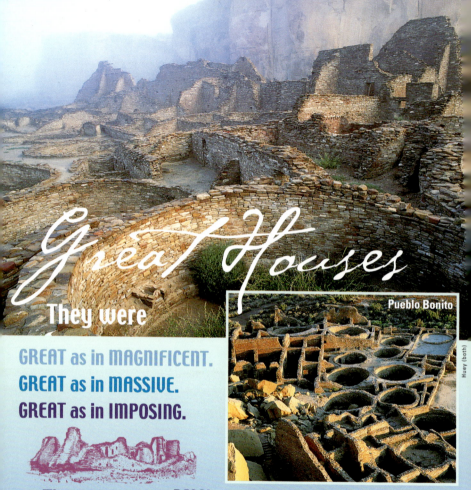

Great Houses

They were

GREAT as in **MAGNIFICENT.**
GREAT as in **MASSIVE.**
GREAT as in **IMPOSING.**

They were almost **REGAL**, as if kings or queens should have owned them. But archeologists believe the Chacoan great houses, with their accompanying great kivas, may not have been for monarchs. Rather, they may represent the work of government and religious officials, some of whom may have had a higher status than others.

Did you know?

Approximately 4,600 archeological sites have been found at Chaco.

Some archeologists suggest that fewer than 2,000 people may have lived at Chaco year-round. They point out that many rooms had no fireplaces. No one would want to sleep in a cold room. SO, why would SO few people need SO much space?

Archeologists believe many of the rooms may have been used as storage. Some have openings that only lead to the outside and not to the interior of the great houses. This suggests that trade was a major part of Chacoan life, and that these rooms contained whatever was traded. What do you think they stored in these rooms?

Archeological dig site

Effigy vessels

Jet frog

Turquoise beads

Doorways at Pueblo Bonito

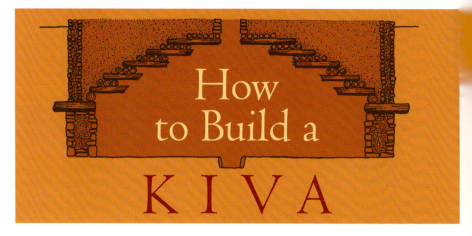

How to Build a KIVA

1. Find a forest.
Kiva builders needed a steady supply of timber, especially tall trees. Support beams for some kiva roofs could be up to 12 feet tall.

Ponderosa pines

2. Find "lumberjacks" able to travel a long way on foot.
The nearest forests, in the Chuska Mountains and on Mount Taylor, were far away from Chaco. Chacoans probably cut the trees, then let them dry before returning home with the logs. A team of people would have worked together to transport logs.

3. Stand 4 massive logs in pits and use them to support the logs that make the kiva roof. Or. . .

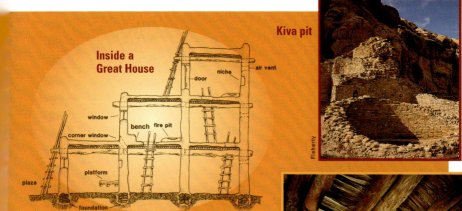

Inside a Great House

Labels: air vent, niche, door, window, corner window, bench, fire pit, platform, plaza, foundation

Kiva pit

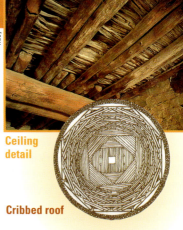

Ceiling detail

Cribbed roof

4. Create a cribbed roof by placing logs on top of 6 or 8 masonry supports, and then position shorter and then shorter logs on top of them, gradually closing the space.

5. Leave a hole at the top for smoke to escape and for people to enter.

6. At the plaza level fill in around the kiva dome with dirt, making the kiva invisible from above.

Did you know?

Chetro Ketl has a colonnade facing the plaza, which is the only one of its kind in Chaco. Was this an idea borrowed from Mexico? Did Chacoans travel to Mexico? Did Mexican people visit Chaco?

Activity slowed down at Chaco nearly 850 years ago, and the Chacoan world began to change – for reasons we will never fully understand. We only know that construction on the great houses stopped and people began to move to places like Aztec and Mesa Verde.

The Chacoans did not disappear. Rather, like clouds, **they reshaped themselves.** Through time **they became** the **Hopi, Zuni, and other Puebloan people of the Southwest.**

In 1849 a Mexican guide from San Ysidro led Lt. James Simpson to Chaco Canyon. An engineer, Simpson immediately recognized its magnificence.

SINCE CHACOAN DAYS

TRAVELING TO CHACO

Pueblo Bonito

Pueblo Bonito

Long ago, people lived all over the Southwest. They enjoyed good food and clean water. When these things became scarce, they moved on. **Life was a series of journeys,** interrupted by periods of settlement. These ancestors read the land like we read books. How did they reach Chaco? How did you?

YOU

You've visited other sites sacred to American Indians. Now you want to see Chaco. You and your parents plan the trip and follow a map. You also read road signs. Once you reach the park, you stop by the visitor center for another map. This shows you how to find places like Pueblo Bonito and Casa Rinconada.

Did you know?

Pueblo Bonito contains more than 650 rooms and 2 great kivas. It was the center of the Chacoan world for 300 years. It is still a sacred place.

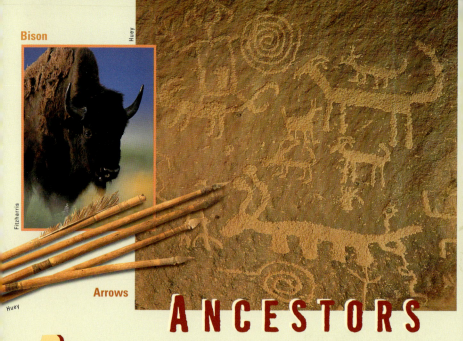

Bison

Arrows

ANCESTORS

As far back as 10,000 years ago people traveled on foot through the Chaco region. They hunted bison and other animals. Later they told stories of their adventures.

As time passed, others tested these stories and followed their tracks back to this region. **Pictures pecked in stone became signposts.** These men and women studied the land to find food and water while they traveled.

They followed other clues too. Landmarks such as **Fajada Butte** and **Chaco Wash** may have guided them. When they reached Chaco, some of them decided to stay.